Pedro Macedo Leão

GERMANY

KEYS TO UNDERSTANDING GERMAN BUSINESS CULTURE

Pedro Macedo Leão

pedromacedoleao@gmail.com

Cover foto:

Skyline in Frankfurt am Main

@Pedro Macedo Leao

© 2011 Lulu Author. All rights reserved.
ISBN 978-1-4478-6295-6

US Trade Format

6 x 9 in./15.24 x 22.86 cm

www.lulu.com

Pedro Macedo Leão

GERMANY

KEYS TO UNDERSTANDING GERMAN BUSINESS CULTURE

Lulupress

"Der Mensch, ein kleines Rädchen im Getrieb des Managements"

"Man, a small gear wheel on the management"

- German proverb

CONTENTS

Introduction

The typical symphony orchestra consists of four proportionate groups of similar musical instruments called the woodwinds, brass, percussion, and strings, and also the fifth proportionate group of similar musical instruments like the rhythm section in modern times.

Among the instrument groups and within each group of instruments, there is a generally accepted hierarchy. Every instrumental group (or section) has a principal who is generally responsible for leading the group and playing orchestral solos. The violins are divided into two groups, first violin and second violin, each with its principal. The principal first violin is called the concertmaster and is considered the leader of not only the string section, but of the entire orchestra, subordinate only to the conductor.

The symphony has a complexity of instruments, precision and timing. In the orchestra each musician contributes with his talent and the combination of different sounds of instruments results in a unique sound. Like a symphony orchestra composed of a large number of performers, the German company also expects that each employee contributes to the success of the whole. Individual responsibility contributes to the group effort. This sense of effort is nurtured and developed by the German education system. This system focuses on efficiency, assigning each a place, but without much freedom to move from one place to another.

Which abilities' needs today a businessman working for a company that claims not only in domestic market but also in the German market?

This book aims to raise awareness of the environment and the German typical errors that can be easily avoided if there is some concern in trying to understand the German mentality, the German market and the situations you will encounter when approaching the market.

Doing business with Germans can be difficult, but it need not be. This guide to doing business in Germany is intended to highlight some important key areas that one may encounter in Germany. After ten years in Germany, I know the country inside out.

Readers should understand that this book, although it concentrates on business culture, is intended to be useful to anybody planning to deal with Germans in any way.

Chapter 1: The Country (Germany)

Germany, officially the Federal Republic of Germany (*Bundesrepublik Deutschland*), is a federal parliamentary republic in Europe. The country consists of sixteen states while the capital and largest city is Berlin.

It covers an area of 357 thousand km2. With 82 million inhabitants, it is the most populous member state and the largest economy in the European Union. It is one of the major political powers of the European continent and a technological leader in many fields.

In summer 1989, Hungary decided to dismantle the Iron Curtain and open the borders, causing the emigration of thousands of East Germans to West Germany via Hungary. This had devastating effects on the GDR – German Democratic Republic, where regular mass demonstrations received increasing support. The East German authorities unexpectedly eased the border restrictions, allowing East German citizens to travel to the West; originally intended to help retain East Germany as a state, the opening of the border actually led to an acceleration of the reform process. This culminated in the Two Plus Four Treaty a year later on 12 September 1990, under which the four occupying powers renounced their rights under the Instrument of Surrender, and Germany regained full sovereignty. This permitted German reunification on 3 October 1990, with the accession of the five re-established states of the former GDR.

Germany was a founding member of the European Community in 1957, which became the EU in 1993. It is part of the Schengen Area and since 1999 a member of the eurozone. Germany is a member of the United Nations, NATO, the G8, the G20, the OECD and the Council of Europe, and took a non-permanent seat on the UN Security Council for the 2011–2012 term. It has the world's fourth largest economy by nominal GDP and the fifth largest by purchasing power parity. It is the second largest exporter and third largest importer of goods. The country has developed a very high standard of living and a comprehensive system of social security. Germany has been the home of many influential scientists and inventors, and is known for its cultural and political history.

Germany has more neighbours than any other European country. Germany is in Western and Central Europe, bordering Denmark in the north, Poland and the Czech Republic in the east, Austria and Switzerland in the south, France and Luxembourg in the south-west, and Belgium and the Netherlands in the north-west.

Countries are like people, with multiple layers, interests, emotions, attributes and desires. Just having a couple of words to describe a country is too simple. Trying to identify the core paradoxes at the heart of the national identity, the attitudes and values of that society should be embraced as a complex task.

Germany has started a series of campaigns "Making Germany sexy" in order to improve the country's image abroad, seeking to replace the stereotypes of "Nazis" and "Sun-bed-stealing-tourists" with a more relaxed, hip and even erotic portrayal of its people and language. The country is trying to shake-off perceptions which they feel have little or nothing to do with the reality of 21st-Century Germany.

German cultural officials want to draw attention to its images celebrities such as the supermodels Claudia Schiffer and Heidi

Klum and sporting heroes like former tennis player Boris Becker and Formula One racing driver Michael Schumacher. It is hoped popular German celebrities will draw attention away from the past. It is hard to change Germany's image, as many of the images associated with the country are too deep-set.

Many German stereotypes - such as the hard working and ruthlessly efficient employee - worked to the country's advantage in the past- even if they no longer match the reality. Country awareness provides instant credibility and identity to new or unknown German brands in new markets. If the value system is coherent, then these products invariably live up to the values of the country of origin. Brands that are not even connected in any way can also reinforce each other. There can be similar expectations associated with buying a Miele dishwasher and a Porsche. The strength and coherence of a system becomes mutually reinforcing brand equity.

I doubt the German brand came out of a strategy brainstorm between the brand managers of Mercedes, BMW, Porsche, Miele and whoever is in charge of the branding of Germany. It is, in the first instance, a truth about Germany and the German people's appreciation of, and attitudes to, technical and functional prowess. What country brands cannot do is manufacture a reputation like this from thin air. It has to be founded on truths and the values of the country which is apparent in the DNA of its export brands.

Chapter 2: The Germans

Otto von Bismarck, a son of the Prussian aristocracy, unified Germany in the 1870s. From 1871 to 1890 Bismarck ruled a unified Germany, modernizing its government and transforming Germany into an industrialized society.

Most Germans still place more importance on regional loyalties, and will rank being German a second after being say, Swabian or Bavarian first.

I don't agree with foreigners that are always complaining about the Germans. I've lived there almost 10 years and can say that the Germans are quite simply misunderstood. If you take a closer look you will come to realize that they are a very polite, shy, fun-loving and humorous people. Don't listen to what others say about the Germans. Go there with an open mind and experience it for yourself. You'll be surprised at the outcome.

Generally speaking, the Germans regard themselves as modest, rather ordinary sort of people. Give them a beer, a *Wurst* (sausage), a bit of *Gemütlichkeit* (cosiness) and another German with whom to argue Aldi promotions of the month or the country's beloved television crime-drama *Tatort* and they will be happy. They are not greedy, do not expect something for nothing and pay their bills on time. Simple and honest *Volk* (people).

For the Germans, life is made up of two spheres: the public and the private. The public sphere of jobs, officialdom and business is radically different from the private one of family, friends, hobbies and holidays. The strict separation of the public from the private provides a guarantee that in private the Germans are open and sincere. They may lack polite cushioning phrases, and keep their distance to strangers and acquaintances much longer than others, but when they accept you as a friend it means that you have made a friend for life.

As a foreigner you will, almost by definition, encounter public Germany first, and may never see more. This explains something of their reputation abroad.

In Germany, life is serious and so is everything else. The Germans strongly disapprove of the irrelevant, the accidental. They value themselves as diligent, thorough, orderly, reliable and methodical. They also see themselves as profoundly well educated. Because life is serious, the Germans go by the rules.

Schiller wrote, "obedience is the first duty", and no German has ever doubted it. This fits with their sense of order and duty. Germans hate breaking rules, which can make life difficult because, as a rule, everything not expressly permitted is prohibited.

The Germans pride themselves on their efficiency, organization, discipline and punctuality. These are all manifestations of *Ordnung* (order). No phrase warms the heart of a German like "*alles in Ordnung*"; meaning everything is all right, everything is as it should be. The categorical imperative which no German escapes is "Ordnung muss sein", order must be.

The German language has two different words for "you." "Du" refers to an informal situation or close friend, and "Sie" refers to a formal situation or a superior. "Sie" is more appropriate when meeting new people. Eventually, the person you are talking to may ask you to use the "du" form, which is a sign of familiarity.

In business never deviate from the formal. When meeting someone for the first time, address them as "Sie". The Germans may remain on "Sie" terms with colleagues even after several years of sharing an office, and a boss calling his secretary by her first name will be suspected of having an affair with her.

The Germans are obsessed with their cars. They love their cars more than almost anything. German cars are pampered, primped and squeaky clean. Only a foreigner would drive around in an unwashed car. Some Germans don't just derive status from their cars; they take their whole sense of identity from them.

2.1 Noise: Silence please *(Ruhe bitte)*

Germans don't mind noise — as long as you don't make any.

I have no solid comparative data to back it up, but I would rate the German tolerance level for noise as among one of the lowest in the world. This is especially true for Germans living next door to you. German ears tend to be highly tuned to noise, especially loud walking and loud partying.

To quote the wonderful German author Kurt Tucholsky (1890-1935): *"Es gibt vielerlei Lärm, aber es gibt nur eine Stille."* ("There are many kinds of noise, but only one silence.")

The preferred German method to control neighbour-noise is called "laws and regulations". German law dictates when and where people can make even normal, everyday "loud" noise, such as lawn mowing. The hours may vary slightly from state to state, but you can see that your lawn-mowing options are very limited, and the kids need to be muted after nine or ten in the evening. The laws and regulations use terms such as Ruhestörung ("disturbing the peace") and Zimmerlautstärke ("room volume"). Apparently, the German term means that you can't make any noise that is loud enough to escape your room and be detected by your neighbours. Of course, considering how sensitive German hearing is, this can be a problem.

When I was living in an apartment in Düsseldorf, the neighbour living on the lower floor send me a letter complaining about my wife walking in high-heels too loud every morning when she was leaving the apartment to work. He explained in his letter that he usually had to work late in the evening and that he needed to rest in the morning. The funny was that my wife didn't have high-heels at all. One letter from the lawyer at the Mietverein and he backed off us instantly. Unfortunately, some people take advantage of foreigners thinking they don't know what their rights are. The law was not that strict concerning noise, especially in morning periods.

It is a good idea to be a member of a Mietverein if you are renting in Germany. Mietverein (Tenants' Protection Union) is an organization to help tenants and offers advice when dealing problems with Landlords. It is probably worth joining one, especially if you predict problems in the future. It doesn't cost very much and could save a lot of stress and money.

Despite the noise laws (or perhaps because of them), German courts are constantly hearing cases of neighbour suing neighbour, or landlord suing tenant over noise issues.

In the past German society as a whole was not well disposed towards children. Children were regarded as noisy and disruptive, liable to interfere with other people's right to quiet and *Ordnung* (order). But times are changing and loud children are no longer considered noise pollution. The German government altered noise pollution laws and made it more difficult to file complaints about the sound of children playing in residential areas. The new regulation will make clear that "the levels of noise from child care facilities and playgrounds are, as a rule, not damaging to the surround environment."

2.2 Humour

Germans love to laugh, but they are badly served by television comedy managers. There is a significant gap between the wit that you can now hear around an urban German dinner table (really!) and the lame, inappropriate jokes served up on TV, both public and private.

German humour refers collectively to the conventions of comedy and its cultural meaning within the country of Germany. Although comedy is a staple of German culture, with many Germans making light of situations in social conversation, and with a large amount of time allotted to comedy in German television broadcasting, it is a widespread stereotype outside the country that Germans have little understanding (or a distorted understanding) of humorous situations. English-language jokes do not translate well because German grammar is less flexible. It does not always allow for a sentence to be reordered so as to delay the punch line, one of the most common joke formats for English speakers. New entities are named by creating compounds, sometimes resulting in extremely long words. This means that fewer words have multiple meanings, so there is less opportunity to create puns. German humour is more prone to make use of local dialects, customs and varieties, which are abundant but less easy to translate. German humour relies more on humorous ideas than on wordplay.

Nevertheless, in German there are a series of jokes based on double meanings, while English uses several words.

> Example from East German political humour: "The train announcer at the main station was imprisoned!" - "Why?" - "He announced 'Please step back' as Erich Honecker's train was arriving!"; in German *zurücktreten, bitte*! can mean both please, step back! as well as please, abdicate!.

Non-German speakers may find understanding German humour difficult, simply due to the language barrier. It is likely that some jokes, puns and humorous turns of phrase would be lost in translation.

2.3 Traditional joke themes and forms

- *Fritzchen* (Little Fritz): A boy of 8-10, who traps adults (usually teachers, parents or policemen) in witty plays of question and answer, exposing their silly or bashful adult ways.

  > Example:
  > Fritzchen and his grandma walk along the pavement. Fritzchen finds a 10 Pfennig coin, but his grandma intervenes: "No, don't pick up anything lying on the ground!" Soon afterwards Fritzchen finds a 10 Mark note, but again his grandma says "No, don't pick up anything lying on the ground!" Soon there is a banana lying on the pavement, grandma steps on it and slips over. "Help me, Fritzchen!", she cries, but Fritzchen says: "No, don't pick up anything lying on the ground!"

- Jokes about other nationals: Germans have their own set of stereotypes about other nations, which sometimes appear in jokes. For example, Scotsmen are portrayed as miserly, Swiss as slow, French as sophisticated lovers, Poles as notorious thieves, the Dutch either as marijuana smokers or slow drivers on motorways (typically with a caravan attached to their car). An Austrian is usually merely an antagonist of a German character, and may be presented as superior, inferior, or an unacknowledged equal.

Example:
The United Nations initiated a poll with the request, "Please tell us your honest opinion about the lack of food in the rest of the world." The poll was a total failure. The Russians did not understand "Please". The Italians did not know the word "honest". The Chinese did not know what an "opinion" was. The Europeans did not know "lack", while the Africans did not know "food". Finally, the Americans didn't know anything about the "rest of the world".

In some respect, the jokes try to be just as in "What nationality was Ötzi the Iceman?" It wasn't Italian, as he carried tools, it wasn't an Austrian, since he had brains, it might have been a Swiss, since he was overtaken by a glacier, but most probably a Northern German, since nobody else walks with sandals in the mountains.

Ötzi the Iceman is the modern name for a well-preserved natural mummy of a man who lived about 5,300 years ago. The mummy was found in September 1991 in the Ötztal Alps, near Hauslabjoch on the border between Austria and Italy. The nickname comes from the Ötztal (Ötz valley), the Italian Alps in which he was discovered. He is Europe's oldest natural human mummy, and has offered an unprecedented view of Chalcolithic (Copper Age) Europeans. His body and belongings are displayed in the South Tyrol Museum of Archaeology in Bolzano, South Tyrol, Italy. Ötzi was found by two German tourists from Nuremberg, Helmut and Erika Simon at the Hauslabjoch, (a mountain pass at 3.210 m height in the Ötztal Alps on the Austrian-Italian border), and excavated by German archaeologist Herbert Hetzel on 19 September 1991; the body was at first thought to be a modern corpse.

- East Frisians (*Ostfriesen*) (East Frisians are a people living in East Frisia, the north-western corner of Germany): This national minority is portrayed as absurdly stupid or naive. Jokes are often in the form of question and answer, both given by the joke-teller.

    Example:
    How many Frisians does it take to screw in a light bulb? Five! One to hold the bulb and four to turn the table he's standing on.
    Example:
    What would you do in case of the Great Flood? Go to East Frisia, because there everything happens fifty years later.

- *Beamte*: German state officials (Beamte). Within jokes, they are considered slow and lazy, doing a nearly useless job in the bureaucracy.

    Example:
    Three in a room and one is working, what's that? - Two officials and a fan.
    Example:

    Three boys argue whose father is the fastest. The first one says: "My father is a race driver, he is the fastest." The second one contradicts: "No, my father is a Luftwaffe pilot, surely the fastest one." "That's nothing.", says the third one. "My father is a Beamter, he is so fast that when work ends at 5 PM, he's already home at 1 PM."

- *Mantawitz* (Manta joke): The male counterpart to the blonde is the *Mantafahrer*, the male driver of an Opel Manta, who is dull, lower class, macho, infatuated with his car and his blonde hairdresser girl friend, and often exceedingly proud and possessive about things that most people would consider embarrassing. Popular in the 1990s.

    Example:
    What does a Manta driver say to a tree after a crash? - "Why didn't you get out of my way, I used the horn!"

- *Antiwitz* (anti-joke): A short, often absurd scene, which has the recognizable structure of a joke, but is illogical or lacking a punch-line.

  > Examples:
  > Two thick feet are crossing the street. Says one thick foot to the other thick foot: "Hello!"
  > "*Zu Fuß ist es kürzer als über'n Berg*" ("Walking is faster than over the mountain").

- Bauernregel (Farmers' rule): Told in the traditional rhyme scheme of weather lore. There are two variants: one is really about weather, but the rule is absurd; the other can be about any other topic, makes some sense, often with sexual connotations, and may feature word play or some real, hidden or twisted wisdom.

  > Examples of the first variant:
  > *Wenn der Hahn kräht auf dem Mist, dann ändert sich das Wetter, oder es bleibt wie es ist.* (When the rooster crows on the dungheap, then the weather will change, or stay as it is)
  > *Wenn noch im November steht das Korn, dann isses wohl vergesse worn* (If in November there is still much crop in the field, then the farmer must have forgotten about it).

  > *Ists an Silvester hell und klar, dann ist am nächsten Tag Neujahr* (If Saint Sylvester's light and clear, the next day'll surely be New Year).

  > *Liegt der Bauer tot im Zimmer, lebt er nimmer* (If a farmer lies dead in a room, he doesn't live no more).

Chapter 3: Learn German – *Sprechen Sie Deutsch?* (Do you speak German?)

Standard German is a West Germanic language and is closely related to and classified alongside English and Dutch languages. Most German vocabulary is derived from the Germanic branch of the Indo-European language family. Significant minorities of words are derived from Latin and Greek, with a smaller amount from French and most recently English (known as Denglish). German is written using the Latin alphabet. German dialects, traditional local varieties traced back to the Germanic tribes, are distinguished from varieties of standard German by their lexicon, phonology, and syntax.

We are the players in a fascinating era, one that interconnects us with others all around the world. With globalization and technology as the driving forces, we find ourselves getting in closer and closer contact with more and more people. Conducting international business in an increasingly competitive market necessitates personal contact; hence more business people are travelling to Germany, which has the largest economy in the European Union.

As a result, knowing how to say at least a few words in a language such as German is becoming an ever-more-vital tool. Unlike Frederick the Great of Prussia, you should be able to speak German.

Frederick the Great of Prussia, who called himself "the first servant of the state," was as much a tyrant as any monarch of the 18th century, but he liked to say of himself that he was "philosopher by instinct and politician by duty." In affairs of state, he was Prussian to the bone, but in language he admired French. He wrote in French, spoke French at his own table ("Since my youth I have not read a German book, and I speak it badly"), once consoled a visiting French intellectual by saying: "You don't know German? You are fortunate in your ignorance."

When discussing with friends and business partners about their experiences in Germany, I often raised the question, "What should one do to get along well in Germany?" I admit I was surprised to find one answer which kept coming back amongst their first suggestions – learn the language!

This advice in some ways runs against the grain because for English speakers living in Germany, it is all too easy not to learn the language. Easy, but not wise – forget what you read in the guidebooks about every German speaking excellent English. There are millions of German residents who can't navigate one complete sentence in English. Still, it is certainly possible to survive in Germany with just English, but you remain sadly limited if you know almost no German and you cut yourself off from a certain level of conversation, communication and general participation in the life of this country. You needn't become a virtuoso in the labyrinthine structures of advanced German, but you should learn at least enough to get along in daily intercourse.

German is a language that few learn for pleasure and none because it is easy. Consequently, anybody who learned German enjoys a special status and a good measure of chic. Few people speak any German, and those who do are seen as exceptional people. I recall attending a trade show in Milan back in the days when I did not speak any Italian. I wanted to ask some questions to a short man at a booth, and asked whether he would rather speak English, French or German. He immediately chose German, although I am quite sure he also spoke some of the others. We spoke in German while his entire colleagues were looking at him in awe, murmuring *Lui parla il Tedesco!* (He speaks German!). This Italian was justly proud of his achievement.

A long-term relationship with the German clients is greatly helped if you speak their language. Germans are demanding but loyal clients. If you speak German, you will get many more clients from Germany than if you could not. Even those Germans who speak some English would much rather trust some person who speaks in German if available.

You should not need to learn any of the numerous German dialects. Every German-speaking region has its own dialect, but usually writes in the regular German (the one you can learn, also known as *Hochdeutsch*). In the North of Germany, the dialect is *Plattdeutsch*, in the South East, *Bayerisch*.

Although in Germany everybody speaks German without problem, in the Swiss-German speaking part of Switzerland many people will be comfortable only in *Schwyzerdütsch*, the local Germanic dialect. *Schwyzerdütsch* is great fun but hard to learn since it is not written and is different in every valley or city.

German grammar is quite tricky, but thanks to several reforms many obsolete grammatical rules have been suppressed and you really get the impression that the Germans have made their best efforts to have as streamlined a language as they could.

The most bothersome aspect of German is that every noun comes with one of three genders (Masculine, Neuter or Feminine), and you really can't predict which gender it is for most of them. Forgetting altogether about the word genders is not an option since everything else in the phrase will depend on the gender.

The structure of the German phrase forces you to wait the end of the sentence to understand the meaning. The fact that many sentence structures place the verb right at the end of the clause means that the listener often has to wait like a frustrated commuter for the meaning of the clause to come along. It also renders the task of simultaneous translation a particularly tricky one. French writer Madame de Stael once complained that it was impossible to have a good conversation in Germany because the grammatical construction of the language always put the meaning at the end of the sentence, and thus made impossible *"the pleasure of interrupting, which makes discussion so animated in France."*

An important basic requisite for rhetoric is vocabulary. The more words you have available, the better you can express yourself. The German language contains about 400,000 words. In the dictionary Duden there are approximately 120,000 words. Your passive vocabulary – these are all words that you understand, but not necessarily use yourself – comprises between 30,000 and 50,000 words. And then there's your active vocabulary – these are all the words that you say at least once over the course of a year. Your active vocabulary contains between 3 and 5 thousand words: Approximately 1/10 (one-tenth) as much as your passive vocabulary. However, there's a step lower than that. The Bild newspaper gets by with about 1000 words. On the other hand, that means that you can express just about anything with 1000 words. Konrad Adenauer, for example, is said to have gotten by with a vocabulary of 1000 words.

The Longest German Word is:

Donaudampfschiffahrtselektrizitätenhauptbetriebswerkbauunterbeamtengesellschaft (Association for subordinate officials of the head office management of the Danube steamboat electrical services).

It is an example of the virtually unlimited compounding of nouns that is possible in many Germanic languages. According to the 1996 Guinness Book of World Records, it is the longest word published in the German language, having 79 letters.

The nature of German grammar is such that compound nouns are a common concept in the language and can be created quite easily. Incidentally, the longest everyday German word still has an impressive 39 letters: Rechtsschutzversicherungsgesellschaften, meaning insurance companies which provide legal protection.

The longest word in any of the major English language dictionaries is pneumonoultramicroscopicsilicovolcanoconiosis, a word that refers to a lung disease contracted from the inhalation of very fine silica particles.

Chapter 4: Names and Titles

One part of learning the German language involves the proper use of German names and titles.

The use of first names is a sign of intimacy and social or professional equality and you should not presume to undermine an elaborate system of mutual respect by suggesting to an elder or superior that you might adopt informal Anglo-Saxon practice.

Germans customarily answer a phone by giving their family names, but much more important is that the caller identifies him or herself fully in the first sentence or two. This is essential for both business and privacy calls, placed before a person's family name are: *Herr* (Mister), *Frau* (Miss, Ms and Mrs.) and *Fräulein* (Miss).

These three terms would and it will do you well to learn this rule quickly.

The three basic terms do nicely to cover all meetings and greetings, except that Germans have an abiding fascination for further titles.

The Germans prize *Bildung*, meaning education. Showing off what you know is not boasting. As evidence, you need merely flip through any Gernan telephone book, to find such educational attainment as *Diplom* (the first college degree) in Engineering, in Economics, etc. None of these achievements is ever appended to a name greeting, but the *Doktor* appellation definitely is. Someone who has earned the doctor's title in any field expects others to acknowledge that fact whenever possible. This means never greeting such a personality with a measly Frau or Herr, but rather *Frau Doktor* or *Herr Doktor*. In addition, some holders of a position such as professor, director, or *Chefarzt* (head doctor, usually also a professor of medicine) count on being addressed with those titles appended to the *Herr* and *Frau*, certainly when they performing their official duties.

Even when filling out Lufthansa's online booking forms, the airline generously provides three levels of academic achievement for its overachieving countrymen: doctor, professor and professor doctor.

Once I met a *Herr Professor Professor Doktor Doktor* - I am not kidding!

Germany's skyrocketing celebrity, Defense Minister Karl-Theodor zu Guttenberg is known for being a blue-blooded baron in demand for red-carpet events next to his well-bred blonde wife Stephanie. Mr. Guttenberg was Secretary of the Economy for a couple of months, and got well know for the episode accusing him that he had plagiarized his doctoral dissertation, forcing him to resign. He rose from the nobility to being the "shooting star" of German politics in less than two years. Guttenberg was a creation of the German media, newspaper BILD in particular. He and his wife knew how to market themselves and orchestrate the media for their purposes. Guttenberg reacted at first by brushing the accusations aside, and then as it had become obvious that it wasn't just a case of a few forgotten footnotes, but that large sections of his dissertation had been copied and at times slightly modified, he reacted with arrogance, followed a few days later by admitting to having made technical errors due to having been overburdened with being a family father and an elected representative. Guttenberg had to resign not only because he plagiarized his doctoral dissertation and thus defrauded the University of Bayreuth, which was bad enough in itself. It was that Guttenberg's public behavior following the disclosures exposed him as a fraud.

The end came when the scientific community got upset about the fact that chancellor Merkel said that what he did was without importance. They felt that if someone whose dissertation is one big fraud isn't punished, then the fundament of science in Germany would have problems. Important scientific institutions protested and he had to resign.

He may have lost his *Doktor*, but still - at least by German standards of etiquette – one has to address him by Herr VON Guttenberg. A title he will never loose, as somehow he never obtained it: it's simply there.

Germany does not have a class system any more. Nowadays nearly everybody belongs to the same class, which could be roughly described as upper-lower-middle-middle class. A small but significant number of German aristocrats do exist. Aristocrats in Germany pass on the parental title to all children. As Germany used to consist of about 300 independent states, each with its own upper class, noble names have always been plentiful. Intermarriages with commoners can spread the name across all class barriers, especially since after a divorce the commoner is entitled not only to keep the title, but to pass it on to future spouses and children as well. This accounts for the astonishing abundance of titles in Germany today.

Chapter 5: Business Meeting

Understanding human need is half the job of meeting them.

- Adlai E. Stevenson

Doing business abroad brings people face to face with different cultures and practices. Prior to travelling to another country it is the norm not to consider factors such as differences in meeting etiquette, negotiation styles and business protocol. However, it is precisely these areas one should be addressing before doing business abroad if the success of the trip is to be given a better chance. A lack of cross cultural understanding leads those doing business abroad to form stereotypes.

The German economy is characterized first and foremost by around 3.6 million small and medium-sized enterprises as well as the self-employed and the independent professions. Some 99.7 percent of all companies are small and medium-sized enterprises. These are firms with annual sales of below EUR 50 million and a payroll of less than 500. Around 70 percent of all those in employment work in this type of company. 48.9 percent of all SMEs operate as service providers, 31.4 percent in manufacturing, and around 19.7 percent in commerce.

Most SMEs are managed by the owners themselves, meaning that the majority shareholder and management of the company are frequently one and the same. Companies are often handed down from one generation to the next. Around 95 percent of German companies are family-owned.

Germany is a tough nut to crack, and there are many examples of multinationals and legions of entrepreneurs who have not been able to deploy in the market. If you want to do business in Germany, not just visit the market quickly and hope that all doors open. The market is very specific and requires a serious commitment. Everyone wants to be present in Germany, and will be difficult to convince them that they really need your products. They already have something similar. Above all avoid selling products developed recently and that have not been adequately tested. Avoid operating instructions and manuals written in English or in a poor German. Many Germans master only their mother tongue, and although it is possible to communicate in English, to enter the market with offers and proposals written in English will put you in disadvantage against companies that approach the market with German. And do not think they are so few! It is common that a German company often receives proposals in their own language.

It should be noted that the opening of Eastern Europe, enabled a large number of new economies to access the German market. When visiting Poland or the Czech Republic, after crossing the border you will find that German is the first foreign language spoken, and that it is very likely that they are not able to communicate in English.

The German buyer, and bear in mind that Germany is a country of buyers - there are buyers in the same company specialized in each type of product - is confronted daily with an abundance of offers both nationally and internationally. He will tend to reject the proposals which do not include the information that he considers necessary. The content of the documentation should be clear, systematic, precise and detailed. Germans value objectivity and love examples. The term "*zum Beispiel*" (for example) is often used. They like facts, facts and more facts and explanatory texts.

Although there is a certain hierarchy, decisions are not concentrated at the top of the hierarchy. The organization is very fragmented and the information does not flow easily between the various departments. Thus, responsibility is usually in the department and is the head of the department that decides on matters assigned to it.

While in many countries a supplier can be chosen quickly and all the details and consequences later analyzed, in Germany is more likely that all details are thoroughly reviewed before any decision is taken. This can frustrate many foreign companies, especially when you are convinced that you have provided enough detail for decision making and find that more research and tests are needed before final decisions are made.

The Germans take decisions at the end of a slow and laborious process, based on extensive research, which means that once a decision has been taken they remain firm and unchanged. Be careful, changing plans after having started a business relationship, can make your German partner nervous.

A typical day begins in Germany earlier than in most other countries and ends sooner. It is very likely that you won't be able to contact someone in the office after 16:00. All important business should be scheduled for early on. At 16:00 your contact in Germany is already mentally preparing to leave. The Friday afternoon are even more problematic since in many companies is no longer possible to talk to anyone.

Find out about the holidays and local festivals like the *Karneval* (carnival) in Cologne or *Oktoberfest* in Munich. Germans enjoy six weeks of vacation per year that are distributed throughout the year and each region has a period suitable for the school holidays. Germans are even known as the "world's travel champions". Not only do Germans have the largest outbound travel market in Europe, they also have the biggest spending on travel. Germans love travelling so much, they even do without other purchases or dig into their savings before giving up their holiday. As travelling is so deeply rooted in the German culture, German workers get lots of annual leave and time to go on vacation. It's quite evident that the tremendous size of the German travel market allows for a wide variety of tourist preferences. There are sun and beach lovers as well as hikers, sportsmen and adventurers, eco-tourists, best agers with lots of different preferences, culture fans, city hoppers, luxury fanatics as well as low budget travelers.

Try to book your meetings well in advance. If arriving late, it is important to call and tell the person who will receive you, providing an acceptable reason for the delay. Remember that punctuality is a serious issue. Business people work hard and are under a lot of pressure. Germans typically plan their time very carefully. It is considered bad etiquette to be late as it shows disrespect for peoples' time.

Germans are often uneasy with uncertainty, ambiguity and unquantifiable risk. This has become manifest in both social and business spheres. Socially, Germans lean towards conservatism and conformism. When doing business in Germany it is possible to notice a heavy emphasis on careful planning, consideration, consultation and consensus. This has developed an appreciation for detail, facts and statistics. Organization is a means of negating uncertainty and averting risk. The emphasis on conformity combined with a fear of the unknown makes Germans very apprehensive about risk. Security is guaranteed through risk analysis. This is achieved through careful deliberation and scrutiny based upon factual evidence as opposed to intuition or 'gut-feeling'. Written documentation is seen as the safest and most objective medium for analysis. A painstaking review of details ensures all relevant information has been taken into consideration. The Germans will analyze proposals thoroughly. Ensure the information you provide is in written format and presented scientifically. Logical conclusions based on empirical evidence will only normally carry any weight. Remember decisions will not be made on your sales technique or charm but on concrete facts that demonstrate a sound opportunity with minimal risk. Decisions are made slowly and methodically. Do not try to rush proceedings or apply pressure. If anything, enquire as to areas in which you may be able to furnish them with additional or more specific information. Try and back-up information with insight from personal experience or professional qualifications. Once a decision has been reached minds are very rarely changed.

Your entry tells others how you expect to be treated. When the receptionist has given you the green light to enter, walk in without hesitation. Do not stand in the doorway like a naughty schoolchild waiting to see the headmaster. When you walk through the door of the person's office, maintain the same speed. People who lack confidence change gears and perform a small shuffle as they enter. When presented to a German, one should seek to maintain the distance; the handshake should be firm and should look his interlocutor in the eyes. Germans believe in the firm handshake which, done properly, should dislocate at least half a dozen of the smaller bones. If someone is crushing your hand in a nice-like grip and won't let go even as stars dance before your eyes and you feel you life-blood ebb, this simply means that they like you.

Moving the chair in an office close to the German client is generally poorly accepted. Fortunately, the German furniture is usually heavy and discourages these movements. Each person has an area or space around him that they claim as his own, as if it were an extension of his body. People react differently when it is invaded and sometimes it is important to keep an 'arms-length' relationship. Our Intimate Zone (between 6 and 18 inches, 15-45cm) is normally entered by another person for one of two reasons: first the intruder is a close relative or friend, or he or she may be making sexual advances; second, the intruder is hostile and may be about to attack. While we will tolerate strangers moving within our Personal and Social Zones, the intrusion of a stranger into our Intimate Zone causes physiological changes to take place within our bodies. The heart pumps faster, adrenalin pours into the bloodstream, and blood is pumped to the brain and the muscles as physical preparations for a possible fight or flight situation are made. This means that putting your arm, in a friendly way, around someone you've just met may result in that person feeling negative towards you, even though they may smile and appear to enjoy it in order not to offend you. Women stand slightly closer to one another, face each other more and touch more than men do with other men. If you want people to feel comfortable around you, the golden rule is 'keep your distance'. The more intimate our relationship is with other people, the closer they will permit us to move within their zones. For example, a new work employee may initially feel that the other staff members are cold towards him, but they are only keeping him in the Social Zone until they know him better. As he becomes better known to them, the distance between them decreases until eventually he is permitted to move within their Personal Zones and, in some cases, their Intimate Zones.

Remember that proper names are reserved for close friends. Titles are of great importance, but the key formula is to use "Herr" (Mr.) for men and "Frau" (Ms.) for the ladies, followed by the family name.

Small talk is not part of German culture; however it is normal that your German business partner ask you about your trip or your country of origin.

Germans value their privacy. Mentally there is a division between public and private life. As a result, Germans wear a protective shell when doing business. Since intimacy is not freely given, this may be interpreted as coldness. However, this is not the case. After a period of time walls and barriers eventually fall allowing for more intimate relationships to develop. People do business with people who make them feel comfortable and it comes down to sincerity and good manners. When entering a foreign country, concentrate on reducing the broadness of your body language until you have the opportunity to observe the locals. A simple way to learn and understand cultural body language differences is to record several foreign films and replay them with the sound off, but don't read the subtitles. Try to work out what is happening then watch again and read the subtitles to check your accuracy.

Avoid the common mistake in the German market to offer all products manufactured by your company, asking "What can we do for you, what do you need? We can provide everything." try to focus on a niche market objectively and focus on the product or service that matters at that particular moment to your German partner.

Try to focus on the reason of your visit and be objective. However, it is likely that situations may arise where the conversation gets more relaxed and you should be careful to the issues you address - the Germans like to discuss and are quite frank but if you don't master the subject try to divert the conversation to issues generally well accepted as sport (usually Formula One and Tennis) or travel holidays. You can be sure that beer is also a great topic of conversation. Germany produces great beer and has many qualities, often produced at regional level. Ask what the typical beer of the region or city where you are and be careful as there are many rivalries - is unthinkable to ask for a *Altbier* (typical beer from Düsseldorf) in Cologne! In Cologne you should ask for a Kölsch.

Former U. S. president Bill Clinton has referred to the phrase "*Ich bin ein Berliner*" (I am a Berliner) and its urban legend when he had visited a pub in Cologne, Germany. When Clinton visited that city on June 1999, he privately and without prior announcement went to a local pub, where he spent two hours, having a typical local meal and chatting to the surprised visitors. Enjoying a glass of the local beer, called *Kölsch*, he allegedly said: "Ich bin ein Kölsch". Unfortunately, in local dialect, the word *Kölsch* stands only for the beer! (He should have said "Ich bin ein Kölner")

Chapter 6: Trade shows (Messen)

Throughout my career I followed the participation of companies in international trade shows and exhibitions. For almost a decade I lived in Germany and regularly visited the major world's trade shows of many and varied sectors.

In this chapter I intend to demystify the difficulties to participate in a trade show and assist all those who have never ventured to do so.

Germany is the World Champion in the organization of trade shows - you can visit trade shows and exhibitions in major cities such as Frankfurt, Dusseldorf, Cologne, Hanover, Munich and Berlin. In fact two thirds of the world's leading trade shows are held in Germany and six in the top ten of exhibition grounds are located in Germany.

In many situations foreign companies come to the German market without having previously held a brain storming on how they intend to establish in the market. The most common approach to the market begins with a trade show booth, performing some contacts, and then the company returns to its country of origin. Major trade shows in Germany are platforms that enable global contacts with buyers from many countries around the world. When the target is to address the German market, not just the presence at the trade show should be considered, but also a lot of preparatory work must be done before the trade show.

The next step allowing a company to better understand the German market is to work with an agent or a distributor in Germany. The idea is to test the company's products in the market in a relatively economic way. The difficulty lies in finding the right person. Usually the relationship with an agent results from a meeting at the trade show, and when the agreement is made, the foreign company sometimes forgets to check whether the person in question has the financial and professional qualifications to market their products. Germany is a big country and the constant traffic jams on motorways make it impossible to work with only one seller across the country. A minimum of five can cover the whole country, but you may choose to focus your initial activity in areas with higher population density and purchasing power.

When you contact German agents or distributors you should have already done your homework. You must have prepared acceptable information, preferably in German, and price lists in Euro. Prices should be calculated for delivery of goods on the client: only large companies are accustomed to working with EX-WORKS price. No one likes this extra work.

Participation in a show might seem a difficult task to perform for those who never became involved in the process.

-   After all what is needed and where to start?

The first difficulty seemed to be the choice of right Tradeshow where to exhibit the products. For a company that has never exported or that has never prospected clients abroad, the choice of the country and the show seem to be something very complex. I suggest as first step to discuss with professionals in your circle of knowledge. In the case of traditional areas of activity for experienced professionals it is relatively easy to identify two or three Trade shows that better suit a first appearance. You may also identify your competitors and seek information on which trade shows they exhibit. The AUMA (Association of German trade show and exhibition sector) has a powerful website www.auma.de where you can find a list of trade shows that are held in Germany but also worldwide.

After choosing the trade shows of interest to participate, you should study the information concerning the profile of the visitors - you can ask directly the organization of the trade show to provide you the visitor's and exhibitor's profile. It is also very important to look into the online catalog of previous editions to assess the importance and notoriety of the trade show and type of exhibitors.

The second difficulty seemed to be how to organize space and build the stand. Many professionals are unaware that trade shows exhibition grounds already have modular stands to sell.

Participating with a modular stand is much easier and less expensive than many people realize. The main exhibition grounds have modular booths to propose to their customers. A modular booth does not project a picture of a well established company in the market and does not contribute for enhancing the image and reputation of a brand. But in the case of a first participation it has the advantage of lower costs and especially to allow more effective control of the budget spent on the construction of the booth.

There are several tricks to enhance a modular stand, but as the aim is to keep costs down, the imagination can contribute to a good end result. Some suggestions: do not use the standard features of the exhibition grounds since in many cases the cost of the rental is close to the cost of buying them. You should choose furniture that makes the most of your products. The imagination can make a difference and the use of lighting techniques, photographic images, fabrics and textures can enhance the stand.

Over the years I contacted many business representatives, who participated as exhibitors in various trade shows and found that many are completely unaware of the universe revolving around the media, especially print media during the trade show. Trade shows have press rooms, equipped with infrastructure and equipment to provide working conditions for journalists who attend the show. These rooms have an area with lockers or shelves where companies can place press kits with information on the activities of the company or products they manufacture. You should take into account that a journalist is someone who actively seeks information and content because he has the obligation to "fill" the pages of one or more publications, according to the importance of the journalist. When registering for a show, you should check with the organization the possibility of using of a box in the press area for your press kit. In many cases you need to reserve and purchase this space well on advance.

The pressroom will have dozens or hundreds of similar dossiers from many other competitors. You should take care to produce something that would attract journalists, whether by color, shape or content. The inclusion of a small giveaway may motivate other journalists who also would like to have the same give-away. The effect of curiosity may result the journalist to question other journalists - "where did you find that gift?" I was always surprised by how people are attracted to small give-aways or gifts. It may also include an invitation to attend your press conference or happy hour on your booth. Keep in mind that journalists are opinion makers and can advertise your company almost for free – you just need to captivate and seduce them!

Chapter 7: Food and meals

Germany, as a nation, is actually very young. Prior to the national unification in 1871, Germany was divided into many kingdoms and principalities, each with distinct customs and even distinct dialects. The sixteen Bundesländer (states) that today make up the Federal Republic of Germany have different specialties.

As the Germans Say, "Eat Breakfast Like an Emperor, Lunch Like a King and Dinner Like a Poor Man." *Abendbrot* is a unique German tradition that involves a light and healthful evening meal shared with family. Literally translated, the word *Abendbrot* means "evening bread," yet the term implies more than eating bread in the evening — it's a simple evening meal in which family comes together and shares the day's news around the table. A traditional *Abendbrot* meal in Germany is served between 6 and 7 p.m. and consists of a selection of whole grain bread, cheeses, deli meats and sausages, mustards and pickles. Often it is accompanied by a salad or a soup, depending on the season. Germans commonly consider it better to eat a smaller dinner such as this — better for the metabolism and a good night's sleep.

A typical breakfast (*Frühstück*) in Germany consists of a warm beverage such as coffee, bread or bread rolls (*Brötchen*) with various spreads and toppings such as butter, jam, *Quark* (a type of curd cheese), sausage and cheese. A glass of juice is also commonplace. Cereals are also popular particularly among younger people. *Müsli*, which is a mixture of cereal flakes, nuts and berries among other ingredients, is one example of a popular cereal. It is mixed with yogurt or milk. With today's busy lifestyles there is a growing trend towards eating a more simple breakfast, so you are more likely to see young people eating cereals rather than tucking into a more hearty meal of bread, cheese and sausage. However, the traditional breakfast of fresh breads accompanied by a cheese or meat selection is still alive and well, particularly at the weekends when the family has more time.

Germans have plenty of words to describe a meal that is eaten between main meals. Far from being unhealthy, eating small snacks between meals is encouraged to prevent overeating at lunch and dinner. Eating a snack between breakfast and lunch is very traditional in German schools and this is called *Pausenbrot* or *Zweites Frühstück* (second breakfast). Since German schoolchildren generally don't eat meals at school, there's quite a long wait between breakfast and lunch, which typically they eat at home. So, the *Pausenbrot* is meant to make sure they have the energy and ability to concentrate for the entire morning. It can be a small sandwich consisting of whole grain bread and cheese or lunch meat. Fruit, yogurt or a *Müsli* bar are also popular *Pausenbrot* snacks.

While children have their *Pausenbrot*, adults also need to keep their energy levels up during the day. For them, it's the *Zwischenmahlzeit* (In-between meal) that keeps them going between meals. A *Zwischenmahlzeit* is also referred to as *Brotzeit*, *Vesper* and *Zweites Frühstück*. The English word Snack is also used, as is *Imbiss*, although these refer more to actual meals that may replace main meals, whereas the *Zwischenmahlzeit* is meant to be eaten in addition to the main meal.

Traditionally, German families eat their main meal during the day, between 12 and 2 p.m. A typical lunch plate might consist of *Kartoffelsalat mit Würstchen oder Frikadellen* (potato salad with sausage or meat balls), *Spätzle mit Geschnetzeltem* (Spätzle noodles with stir-fry), *Schnitzel mit Buttergemüse* (Schnitzel with buttered vegetables) or *Fischstäbchen mit Kartoffelpüree* (Fish sticks with mashed potato). Meat is served most every day, particularly pork. Vegetables are also a standard part of any *Mittagessen*. Typical vegetables served at lunchtime are *grüne Bohnen* (green beans), *Möhren* (carrots), *Erbsen* (peas) and *Kohl* (cabbage). Potatoes are also a staple and come in the form of *Salzkartoffel* (boiled), *Knödel* (dumplings), *Bratkartoffel* (fried potatoes), *Krokette* (croquettes), *Kartoffelpüree* (mashed potatoes) and of course, *Pommes Frites* (french fries). Of course, as popular as potatoes are, rice and noodles are also eaten as side dishes.

Kaffee und Kuchen literally means "Coffee and Cake" and it's very similar to the English tradition of "Teatime". It's a custom that brings families together to enjoy a little "*Gemütlichkeit*" (a word that means coziness). Families and friends gather together in the mid to late afternoon to drink coffee and enjoy a slice of cake. Typical cakes you might find at such a gathering include *Schwarzwälderkirschtorte* (Black Forest cake), *Bienenstich* (bee sting cake), *Käsekuchen* (cheesecake made with Quark) and fruit tarts such as *Zwetschenkuchen* (plum tart). You can also purchase pastries from the corner *Bäckerei* (bakery) such as *Mohnstückchen*, a poppy seed pastry and *Apfeltasche*, an apple-filled strudel-type pastry pocket. The cakes and pastries are, of course, almost always accompanied by a steaming hot cup of rich German coffee with cream or condensed milk. However, tea has become more popular over the last decade, particularly in Ostfriesland, where it has always been traditional and where a quarter of all the tea in Germany is consumed.

The most typical Fast Food meals eaten in Germany are similar to those eaten in American namely burgers, pizza and fries from well-known chains such as Macdonald's, Burger King and Pizza Hut. Other popular meals are *Bratwurst*, served with a bread roll, *Currywurst* (a sliced sausage served with a curry-flavored ketchup sauce and *Pommes* (French fries) served either with mayonnaise or ketchup or sometimes with both! This combination is called *Pommes rot-weiss* referring to the red ketchup and the white mayonnaise. The sausages and fries can all be purchased from street stalls known as *Würstchenbuden*. One of the most common Fast Food meals that has risen in popularity is the *Dönerkebab*, which was first introduced in Germany by Turkish immigrants. You'll find a *Dönerbuden* (kebab) on many street corners in large cities and towns. A *Dönerkebab* is made from lamb or veal slices cut from a rotating vertical roasting spit. The meat is served in a warm pita pocket or flatbread (*Fladenbrot*) along with lettuce, onion, cucumber, tomatoes and a yogurt sauce.

7.1 At a restaurant:

- Unless it is a fancy restaurant you don't usually have to wait to be seated. You can just find a table that is free.

- Feel free to sit with strangers in a restaurant, once you determine *"ob hier noch frei ist?"* (Is this place free?)

- Don't expect ice cubes in soda, you need to ask for it.

- If water is desired, it is almost always bottled Mineralwasser (sparkling mineral water), not out of the tap. If you don't want the fizzy stuff, ask for "stilles Wasser".

- Doggiebags are still mostly unknown so your waiter/tress may be surprised if you asked to take leftovers home with you.

- Tips are not usually generous, since German wait staff are usually well paid and don't rely on tips for their wages. A general rule is to round up the bill, so if your bill is, say 22.50 Euros you might give 24 or 25. You may find that your waiter/waitress will remain at the table while you pay, so make sure to let them know how much tip you want to leave.

- Credit cards are not accepted in all the restaurants, it is more usual to pay with cash. Trendy restaurants that are always busy usually don't accept them. It can come as a rather nasty surprise to suddenly discover that the nice restaurant you just dined in does NOT accept credit cards. Many restaurants in the German-speaking world, even some very fine ones, do not accept credit cards of any kind. It is wise to always check about plastic payment — before you order. If you don't see any credit card logos—the familiar-looking ones for Visa, MasterCard, American Express, etc.—then be sure to ask the waiter

7.2 At the dinner table:

- Make sure you say "*das schmeckt*" - it tastes good.

- When eating or drinking together, wait until someone says "*Guten Appetit*" or wants to "*anstossen*" (click glasses to say "cheers").

- Germans don't put their hand on their lap while eating and it's considered rude to put your elbows on the table.

- Germans tend to eat less with their fingers so use a fork to eat your fries.

- They also eat with both knife and forks so don't just use your knife to cut your food and then only use your fork.

- If you cross your knife and fork on your plate, it means you are just pausing. If you lay your knife and fork side by side, it means you are finished, and the waiter may come and take your plate away.

7.3 Bread

Bread is taken very seriously in Germany. High street bakers flourish and varieties abound. What is even more impressive is that German breads tend to be of the healthy wholegrain type, packed with flavor and nutrients. The most popular breads include rye flour either with or without wheat. Rye flour has low levels of gluten and so the texture tends to be denser. Wheat is added to give a lighter texture and a good crust. Seeds and whole grains are popular additions for flavor and texture and, of course, regional variations means breads come in many shapes and sizes. Darker rye breads have a moist and chewy texture and store for a good length of time without going stale. They are a particularly good way to start the day at breakfast time topped with thinly sliced cheese and ham.

7.4 *Brezel* – (Pretzels)

Fresh pretzels have a dark, salty crust and delicious chewy bagel-style texture. They are easy to eat on the run as they are clean and not messy. They are made with yeast which smells and tastes so nice. They are absolutely wonderful at the beer fest with a stein full of cold '*Kellarbier*', great with butter on, the list goes on and on. I think some German children could say the word 'Brezel' before they could say Mum. A Brezel is that weird looking knot thing that you see in the bakeries by their thousands.

7.5 *Spargelzeit* – Asparagus Season in Germany!

April marks the beginning of *Spargelzeit*, asparagus season, in Germany. The first crop is harvested around mid-April and the season runs through the feast of St. John the Baptist, June 24. Whereas the tender vegetable, especially the green variety, is increasingly available in supermarkets year-round, in Germany asparagus still is a distinctly seasonal product. Just as apples mark the fall season, nothing epitomizes spring quite like this revered white stalk. Germans prefer the white variety. The main difference between white and green asparagus is the way they are grown which affects the vegetable's color and flavor. White asparagus grows entirely surrounded by earth which protects the slender stalk from sunlight exposure and thereby keeps it from turning green. Soil is piled up into knee-high banks giving asparagus fields their characteristic appearance. It takes three years for a plant to produce its first tip. The popular vegetable grows best in sandy soil and is cultivated in almost all federal states as well as in neighbouring countries. Asparagus is valued for its delicate flavor but also for its high nutritional value. Rich in nutrients and very low in calories, asparagus is indeed a very healthy food.

The states of Baden-Württemberg and Lower Saxony take special pride in being prime asparagus growing regions and both states are home to scenic "Asparagus Routes". The Baden route runs through the towns of Schwetzingen, Reilingen, Karlsruhe and Rastatt. The city of Schwetzingen claims to be the "Asparagus Capital of the World" and like many of the towns along these routes it holds an annual *Spargelfest* (asparagus festival) which attracts visitors from near and far. During these festivals asparagus aficionados can get their fix of delicious fresh asparagus dishes and enjoy plenty of entertainment including the popular peeling contests. The most prominent of these festivals crown an asparagus queen or king.

During asparagus season, the average German enjoys the delicate flavor of this tender spring vegetable at least once a day which adds up to a national total of over 70,000 tons per year. With annual production averaging less than 60,000 tons, Germany also imports asparagus to meet the continuously high demand for the healthy stalks. The vegetable's popularity may in part be rooted in its long history as a luxury vegetable. Going back as far as 2000 BC, the prized vegetable was cultivated by the Ancient Egyptians, the Greeks and the Romans. During the rule of the French Sun King, Louis XIV, it gained in popularity and was reserved to the tables or the courts. The first document which mentions the cultivation of asparagus in the region around the city of Stuttgart dates back to the 16th century.

When buying asparagus, freshness is the key to the perfect flavor and texture. Gourmets know that it tastes best "picked in the morning, eaten at midday". Make sure the stems are firm, crisp and plump, and have the characteristic velvety sheen. The tips should be intact and firm, a slight purple tinge is normal. If you don't intend to cook them right away, wrap them in a damp kitchen towel and store in the refrigerator's crisper. Preparing asparagus always start with washing the stalks, followed by peeling them with a swivel vegetable peeler. White asparagus is peeled downwards starting just below the tip, whereas green asparagus is usually peeled from bottom towards the tip. The more serious asparagus aficionados keep a special steamer handy which is supposed to help cook the vegetable as gently as possible, preserving more of its flavor. The steamer pots are either slender and tall or shallow and oval-shaped. When using a normal pan, a good trick is to tie the stalks together using kitchen twine. The most common preparation calls for cooking the vegetable in water for about 12-15 minutes, depending on the thickness of the stalks. The water may be flavored beforehand by adding some butter, salt, a pinch of sugar and the stems and peel left over from peeling.

Asparagus season gets the creative culinary juices flowing and in Germany practically every restaurant features the tasty vegetable prominently on their menu. The most popular ways of enjoying white asparagus are deliberately simple so as not to overpower the vegetable's delicate flavor: served with melted butter and new potatoes (*Spargel mit Butter*), with ham (*Spargel mit Schinken*) or with hollandaise sauce (*Spargel mit holländischer Sauce*). For the more adventurous fans of this quintessential spring vegetable, Germany's innovative chefs are constantly coming up with new ways to serve the tender stalks as an appetizer, entrée or even as part of dessert.

Chapter 8: Culture and conversation themes

Capital "C" Culture is not everybody's cup of tea. In business conversations I always had difficulty in introducing themes like Fritz Lang movies or Thomas Mann books.

Germany's history is a traumatic and collectively difficult area of conversation. Germany remains uneasy over its history, even among the younger generation. This is a subject that it is best not to approach unless your German host takes the lead. Making jokes about German history is a definite no, and Germans will not take kindly to this. Germans are ashamed of their country's history, and will feel as if they are being mocked.

Here are some topics that I believe can provide much better results and may be the best for small talk with your German business partners. Knowing that you are aware of their favourite television shows, Christmas traditions or *Prominente Leute* (famous people) will create a warm atmosphere.

Aldi

ALDI, short for "Albrecht Discount", is a discount supermarket chain based in Germany. The earliest roots of the company trace back to 1913, when the mother of Karl Albrecht and Theo Albrecht opened a small store in a suburb of Essen. Their father was employed as a miner and later as a baker's assistant. Karl Albrecht was born in 1920, Theo in 1922. The chain is made up of two separate groups, ALDI Nord (North - operating as ALDI MARKT), headquartered in Essen, and ALDI Süd (South - operating as Aldi Süd), headquartered in Mülheim an der Ruhr, which operate independently from each other within specific market boundaries. The individual groups were originally owned and managed by brothers Karl Albrecht and Theo Albrecht; Karl has since retired and is Germany's richest man. Theo was Germany's second richest man until his death in July 2010. Aldi's

German operations currently consist of Aldi Nord's 35 individual regional companies with about 2,500 stores in western, northern, and eastern Germany, and Aldi Süd's 31 regional companies with 1,600 stores in western and southern Germany.

Aldi weekly newsletter of special prices called *Aldi informiert* ("Aldi informs") is distributed in stores, by direct mail, and often printed in local newspapers. This newsletter is a must in Germany and always a topic of conversation in companies.

Bayreuther Festspiele or "The Bayreuth Festival"

Is a music festival held annually in Bayreuth, Germany, at which are presented performances of operas by the 19th century German composer Richard Wagner. Performances take place in a specially designed theatre, the Bayreuth Festspielhaus. The Festival has become a pilgrimage destination for Wagner enthusiasts, who often must wait years to obtain tickets. The event has become a must for Germany's politicians and jet-set, who pay several hundred Euros for tickets.

Claudia Schiffer

Known as one of fashion's top models, the tall, Teutonically blonde Mannekin from Düsseldorf is also one of the world's richest. Discovered by German designer Karl Lagerfeld in 1988, Schiffer announced in October 1998 that she would retire from the fashion runway. She continues to do photo and ad work, and make TV appearances.

Cherished German Christmas Traditions

Advent Season

The Christmas season in Germany begins four Sundays before Christmas Eve with the start of Advent. The Advent season and its celebration have changed over the years from being quite serious to one of a more joyous nature - where we receive treats like chocolate-filled Advent calendars. The tradition is meant to count down the four weeks leading up to Christmas Eve. The Advent or Christmas calendar began as a plain card with paper backing. On the face were 24 windows that when opened revealed various Christmas symbols and scenes. Today the most popular version of this calendar is the candy-filled variety. Instead of mere pictures, the windows open to reveal pieces of chocolate shaped to resemble stars, angels, fir trees, and other Christmas symbols.

Weihnachtsmarkt or **Christmas markets**

During Advent season the historic city centers of every major German city and many smaller towns light up with holiday decorations and lure locals and tourists alike with vendors of local arts and craftsmanship, plenty of great food and the ubiquitous Christmas market beverage - *Glühwein*. The Christmas market tradition (*Christkindlmarkt* or *Weihnachtsmarkt* in German) dates back to the 15th century. Today over 2500 Christmas markets all over Germany invite visitors to get into the festive mood. The market is usually located on the city's central square and commonly features a nativity scene; bigger cities might offer a central stage for traditional musicians and dancers. Vendors offer a wide range of gifts that are often still handcrafted, as well as a mouthwatering array of grilled sausages and meats, fried fish filets on a fresh bread rolls, sautéed mushrooms, and an unending variety of specialty sweets, confections and baked goods. Christmas markets are a treat for all the senses - beautiful to behold, delicious scents wafting through the air and a definitive feast for the taste buds.

The Nuremberg or *Nürnberger Christkindlmarkt* is the most famous Christmas market in Germany, with over 2 millions visitors from all over the world yearly. About 180 wooden stalls, festooned with red-and-white cloth, have given the Christmas Market its name of "Little Town from Wood and Cloth". *Christkindlmarkt* is translated literally as "Christ Child Market" and the *Christkind* is considered an essential part of this particular market. The *Christkind* or Christmas Angel is elected every two years and has to be a girl, aged between 16 and 19 years old. The selection is taken very seriously; there is even a jury to select the finalists, whittled down from a huge number of competitors on an internet poll. Every year, on the Friday before the first Advent Sunday, the *Christkind* opens the *Christkindlmarkt* with a prologue. The Christmas market is spread all over town with stalls sporadically placed leading up to *Hauptmarkt*, the square right in front of the *Frauenkirche* (Church of the Lady). The *Hauptmarkt* is, so to say, the centre of the old town and also the centre of the *Christkindlmarkt*. Authentic Elisenlebkuchen; premium quality Lebkuchen (a soft, German version of gingerbread) can be only found in Nuremberg. It is designated the Protected Designation of Origin by EU law and must be produced within the boundaries of the city.

Glühwein

On a cold day, nothing will warm you up faster than a mug of steaming *Glühwein*. This quintessential Christmas market beverage consists of hot mulled red wine, with an optional shot of brandy (*Glühwein mit Schuss*). Most major cities in Germany serve *Glühwein* in ceramic mugs specifically designed for the local Christmas markets. Similar to the practice in Bavarian beer gardens, when purchasing *Glühwein*, you will pay a deposit on top of the price of the beverage. Once finished, this gives you the option of either returning the mug to get your deposit back or keeping it as a nice souvenir. While the designs vary, the mugs usually depict either the respective historic city centers or the Christmas market.

Gift Giving - *Sankt Nikolaus* and *Christkind*

The day of *Sankt Nikolaus* revolves exclusively around children. On his Saint's Day, December 6, *Sankt Nikolaus*, the German version of Santa Claus, helps ease children's eager anticipation during the pre-Christmas season. The night before December 6, children in Germany will place a freshly polished pair of boots in front of their bedroom doors. Upon waking up they find them stuffed with fruit, nuts and candy. Originally it was *Sankt Nikolaus* who was in charge of gift giving on the night before his saint's day December 6. With the Reformation came a movement away from the worship of saints, and the tradition of giving and opening gifts was moved to

Christmas Eve. Gifts have since been brought by the Christkind or "Christ Child" and are usually opened after a traditional family meal and the singing of Christmas carols.

Christmas Foods

The traditional holiday meal consists of duck, goose, rabbit or a roast, accompanied by well-known Germany delicacies, including apple and sausage stuffing, red cabbage, and potato dumplings. One of the most famous German delicacies is *Stollen*. Since 1329, this unique "fruitcake" has been considered one of the most precious Christmas pastries in the world. The most famous kind of *Stollen*, which can be found at most local supermarkets, is called *Dresdner Stollen*, originating from the German city of Dresden. This tasty version bursts with nuts and fruit and is sure to change your mind about the term "fruitcake." *Stollen* is shaped with tapered ends and a ridge down the center, symbolizing the Baby Jesus in swaddling clothes, in which it was customary to wrap newly born children.

Der Schuh des Manitu or "Manitou's Shoe"

One of the best German films of all time? Well, funny he is. I think many Germans must have seen the movie 1000 times.

"Der Schuh des Manitu" is a 2001 German parody of western films. Parodies a series of Wild West adventure novels of the 19th century German author Karl May. The main topic of these novels is the deep friendship of a fictional Apache chief (Winnetou) and his white settler companion and blood-brother, (Old Shatterhand), who are both exemplary virtuous and stand together to keep the peace between Indians and immigrating White settlers. *Der Schuh des Manitu* spoofs the friendship motif in the Winnetou novels and in their 1960s film adaptations which has largely led to high, but sometimes idealised and cliché ridden admiration of Native Americans in Germany.

Directed by Michael Herbig, it is a film adaptation of the Winnetou sketches from his Pro Sieben television show *Bullyparade*. The movie is the most financially successful German movie. The movie borrows from the parodies of Mel Brooks like *Robin Hood: Men in Tights*, *Blazing Saddles*, and *Dracula: Dead and Loving It*. Its humor consists largely of blatant anachronisms, scenes such as the character Ranger getting stopped by a sheriff for "fast riding" and being asked for his "riding license", or Santa Maria connecting the dots on a map by using a feather with a marker-tip. Greek character Dimitri owns a mule named Apollo 13 (his twelve brothers - and subsequently, he as well - were killed by speeding trains), and for lack of a hatchet the Shoshones, a Native American tribe, dig out a folding-chair they had buried.

The movie has several references to the Karl May movies of the 1960s and to Herbig's own TV show. It features many puns that are difficult to translate into English. In the German version, Abahachi, Ranger and Winnetouch all speak with a rather strong Bavarian accent that is predominant in the Bullyparade-Show, which is mentioned by the barkeeper at the saloon by *"You must be Ranger, the man with the Southern States accent"*.

Many scenes have been shot in Almería, Spain, at the same places that can be seen in many movies of Sergio Leone. Most of the Indians in the movie are actually Spanish. The Shoshone chief is played by an East Indian, for humorous effect, and his two advisors are Native Americans. According to Herbig's comments, some Spanish can be heard on the DVD, and he was never entirely sure if the Spanish actors really knew what kind of movie they were participating in. The Mexican Hombre is played by Hilmi Sözer, a Turkish-German actor.

Die Sendung mit der Maus or "The Show with the Mouse"

Children's television programme. The orange-colored mouse with no name debuted on March 7, 1971 on western German regional public broadcaster WDR, and has been delighting tiny viewers since with his educational explanations of day-to day questions. One of the secrets to the success is that we take children seriously and always adhere to the approach that there are no dumb questions. The 30-minute show, which also features a tiny blue elephant, a yellow duck and a cuddly seaman Captain Blue Bear, now airs every Sunday at 11:30 am on national public broadcaster ARD and children's channel Ki.Ka. Having gained cult status, the show garners some 1.6 million viewers each weekend - many of whom grew up watching the show in the 1970s and now watch with their own children.

Dieter Bohlen

More than two decades after Modern Talking, Dieter Bohlen still gets Germany going. He is a regular in the gossip columns and in particular, he is the powerhouse behind the fifth season of "Germany Seeks a Superstar." In the German version of the original British TV Idol franchise, the musical abilities of the candidates are much less interesting than whether or not Bohlen is going to behave objectionably again. Bohlen, 54, is the ratings hit's only constant factor. Dieter Bohlen loves to talk about the most intimate details of his life in public. When watching Dieter Bohlen rating the candidates on TV mega hit "Germany Seeks a Superstar," don't be surprised if you hear all sorts of analogies from the animal kingdom, below-the-belt verbal abuse and a full charge of scatological commentary.

He once said that a candidate sang "like a cow taking a dump," another "like a drunken woodpecker" and the third, "like a sow in her pen." Others sound like they have "a toilet scrubber up their bum," like "a tongue-tied fart" or simply "shit." Bohlen's original claim to fame was his music. With Modern Talking, Blue System and a whole array of other projects, he has sold more than 160 million records around the world. He has loved being in the spotlight since then, and wants to keep it pointed at him at any price. His relationship with Bild, the largest, most powerful tabloid in Germany, is almost symbiotic. The paper enthusiastically prints his slips of the tongue for a circulation in the millions - only to lead the chorus of the indignant a few days later – until the next uproar. Bohlen secures circulation, and in turn, Bohlen, obsessed with his image, assures himself of his own existence through his permanent presence in the media. But the man is an expert and his judgment is incorruptible. If you go by the sales figures, Bohlen is the most successful music producer in Germany. Dieter Bohlen is a German songwriter, singer, musician, producer, entertainer, TV personality, and writer. Bohlen is best known for being part of popular pop-duo Modern Talking around 1985. Bohlen has also released five books. Two of these are autobiographical and describe his career, romantic involvements and experiences with singers. The first book was an unprecedented success in Germany.

Bohlen was married to Erika Sauerland from 1983 to 1994 and has three children from this marriage, Marc, Marvin Benjamin and Marielin. Even before he was legally divorced, he lived with his new girlfriend Nadja Abd el Farrag, nicknamed Naddel. In 1996, he married model and singer Verona Feldbusch but divorced her after thirty days, propelling Verona to celebrity status (she went on to host television shows such as Peep and Veronas Welt). Later, Bohlen lived with the 1979 born model Stefanie Küster. They have one son, Maurice, born mid-2005. He met his current girlfriend Carina in Majorca, Spain, where one of the casting events for Deutschland sucht den Superstar was held. Amelie, was born in 2011, their first child together and Bohlen's fifth child. Bohlen lives in the village of Tötensen near Hamburg.

EC Karte

Expats in Germany already know that Germans just don't use checks. The German equivalent of a personal check is called *eine Geldüberweisung* "money transfer", but these days you rarely see the paper variety. Usually, you handle an *Überweisung* by computer, transferring funds from your German bank account to someone else's account.

Then there's the matter of credit cards. While the US could be termed a cashless (plastic) economy, Germany is definitely a cash economy. Credit cards are not popular in Germany at all. As long as you stick to the tourist circuit (hotels, car rental, travel services, restaurants, etc.), credit cards will usually be accepted (but there are exceptions even here). However, if you are living in Germany "on the economy," as they say, you'll quickly discover that Visa, MasterCard, and American Express are not commonly accepted in many places. Your daily shopping will require cash or an EC card (a type of German debit card). The neighbourhood grocer and even larger supermarkets generally say "nein" to credit cards. While department stores, larger stores, and shopping malls usually accept plastic payment, many will only take an EC card. German bookstores are notorious for not accepting credit cards, but most allow EC card payment.

Harald Schmidt

Harald Schmidt is a German comedian and television entertainer best known as host of two popular German late-night shows *Verstehen Sie Spaß?* and *Die Harald Schmidt Show. Die Harald Schmidt Show* is a late night television show which was broadcast on ARD and hosted from 2004 until 2007. The program was initially aired around 11 pm on Wednesdays and Thursdays by Das Erste, one of Germany's public broadcast stations. An episode of *Harald Schmidt* lasted 30 minutes. The show was recorded in Studio 449 in Cologne-Mülheim in front of an audience or broadcasted live.

Heidi Klum

Heidi's father had earlier been a production manager for the 4711 perfume company. She grew up in her birthplace of Bergisch Gladbach, a medium-sized city just outside Cologne. Klum's modeling career began while she was working as a barmaid in a Düsseldorf discotheque in 1992. A girlfriend (Karin) encouraged the then 18-year-old student to enter a German TV talent show called "Model '92." The show, sponsored by the German women's magazine Petra, was part of a late night talk show hosted by Thomas Gottschalk. Klum competed against 25,000 contestants from all over Germany and Europe until she was one of three semifinalists. In April 1992 she won the top $300,000 modeling prize.She signed with Metropolitan, a German modeling agency, and successfully modeled in Europe before going to the United States in 1993. Her biggest success there came when she began working for Victoria's Secret. Klum's career was now reaching a level which opened up more opportunities, including putting her name on her own lines of perfume, clothing, jewelry, and Birkenstock shoes. From there she moved on to films and television. She also has lucrative contracts for print and TV advertising for firms such as Douglas (a German retailer), McDonald's and Volkswagen in Germany and the US.

Heidi Klum's personal life has not always gone as smoothly as her career. In 1997 she married celebrity hairstylist Ric Pipino, an Australian of Italian heritage living and working in New York City (cuts from $110 to $300). Their marriage lasted five years. After her 2002 divorce, Klum dated Italian businessman (Formula One racing) Flavio Briatore. In 2003, she announced she was pregnant by Briatore. On the day of her announcement Briatore was photographed kissing Fiona Swarovski, an Austrian jewelry heiress. Klum and Briatore parted soon thereafter. Klum was still pregnant when she met British-born singer-songwriter Seal, of Nigerian and Brazilian heritage. Klum and Seal were married in Mexico on May 10, 2005. They have three children: a daughter and two sons. Seal officially adopted Leni, Klum's daughter by Briatore, in December 2009. Since November of that same year, Klum's legal name has been Heidi Samuel, after she took the surname of her husband. In 2008 Klum became a naturalized US citizen, according to her, in order to be able to vote for Barack Obama for president that year. Klum visits her German homeland and her family there as often as she can. She says that she feels at home in both Los Angeles and Bergisch Gladbach. She is often a guest on American and German talk shows.

Herbert Grönemeyer

Herbert Grönemeyer's "Mensch" album (2002) remains the best-selling album of all time in the German market, able to reach the top of the German music charts with the hit singles Männer "Men" and Flugzeuge im Bauch "Airplanes in my stomach". For the FIFA World Cup games in Germany in 2006, Grönemeyer composed and recorded the official anthem Zeit, dass sich was dreht "Celebrate the Day". Earlier, for the 2004 Olympic Games in Athens, he had done the same with the anthem "Everlasting." His recent albums include "12," which won an Echo for Best Album of the Year, and the retrospective Was muss muss. He also re-released albums by the German electronic pioneers Neu! Germany's best-known singer and musician has been living and working in London since 1998.London has proved to be a creative reservoir for Grönemeyer. In the British capital he has been working with British producer Alex Silva. The result has been three of Grönemeyer's best albums: *Bleibt alles anders*, Zwölf and, most notably, Mensch. More recently, Grönemeyer appeared in the 2007 British film Control, helmed by the Dutch director Anton Corbijn. It was that association that led to Grönemeyer composing the music for Corbijn's Hollywood film, The American (2010), starring George Clooney, Violante Placido and Thekla Reuten.

Karneval or Fasching

Dating back to the Middle Ages, the celebration of Carnival (*Karneval* or *Fasching*) is a time for eating, drinking and merriment before the solemn days of Lent. This colorful festival takes place for one week, starting 52 days before Easter, generally ending with a bang in time to calm down for Ash Wednesday. Carnival is celebrated in several regions throughout Germany, the two most popular versions being *Karneval* with its hub in the *Rhineland* region and *Fasching* (also *Fastnacht*) in Southern Germany.

Fastnacht season begins on Three Kings Day, January 6 (Epiphany) and is a more subdued celebration observed in cities and rural areas of *Baden-Württemberg* and Bavaria. Costumes have evolved around themes of dark ghosts representing the cold season contrasted by the bright, colorful spirits of spring. These traditional themes symbolize the eager anticipation of the growing season, a time farmers and consumers long for.

Carnival season officially starts much earlier, on November 11th at 11:11 am. At this time people celebrate the beginning of what is often referred to as the Carnival season. In the weeks leading up to the festivities, Carnival clubs meet to discuss upcoming performances, costumes, and parades. The undisputed Carnival capital is Cologne, followed by Düsseldorf and Mainz.

Carnival is traditionally kicked off on Thursday with "Women's Carnival" (*Weiberfastnacht*). On this unofficial holiday women dress up in costumes and misbehave in harmless ways, thus symbolically taking control for a day. A popular tradition is to cut off men's ties, leaving only a short stump of this perceived token of male supremacy. In return the male victims are usually rewarded with a peck on the cheek.

The Monday following Women's Carnival is called Rose Monday (*Rosenmontag*). This day marks the peek of Carnival season, with 11:11 a.m. as the official kick-off time for the popular parades. With excitement and anticipation, people line up along main street to wait for the parade to pass by. The floats are works of art portraying a variety of themes and usually focus on what's happening in the world; for example, one float may make fun of a contemporary governmental leader or recent political event. After the parade wild and free-roaming marchers dressed in crazy costumes (*Narrenkostümen*) gather in the side streets to continue the celebration. Bars stay open through the early hours of morning and the spirit of Carnival reigns in the streets and public squares, in offices and at home, and above all in places for dancing and drinking. To accompany this great fun, street vendors offer simple German fare to keep Carnival enthusiasts happy. On every corner one can buy fresh pretzels (*Bretzel*), hot sausages (*Bratwurst*) or *Krapfen*, the German answer to donuts, and enjoy mugs of hot-spiced wine (*Glühwein*) which helps the Carnival crowd stay warm.

The Tuesday after Rose Monday marks the last day of the carnival season and is observed with smaller parades and parties in Germany. For carnival enthusiasts in other parts of the world, however, Shrove Tuesday, also known as Fat Tuesday or Mardi Gras in French marks the highlight of the carnival season. In cities such as New Orleans, Venice and Rio de Janeiro cheerful and colorful crowds take over the streets with spectacular parades. Ash Wednesday marks the end of the year's craziest "season" and ushers in the solemn weeks of Lent.

Konrad Adenauer (1876–1967)

The Christian Democrat was the first Chancellor of the Federal Republic of Germany. He was head of government from 1949 until 1963. As a result of his unflinching West-oriented policies he integrated Germany into the international community, NATO and the European Economic Community (EEC). His achievements also include reconciliation with France and his attempts at reconciliation with Israel.

Laternenfest

This is a popular children song sing in Germany for St. Martin's Day in November. Children are carrying lanterns they made themselves and singing *Laternenlieder. Laternen Fest*, or "Feast of lanterns", also called "*Sankt Martins Tag*" (Saint Martin's Day). Saint Martin of Tours was a Roman soldier who converted to Christianity and spread his faith across Europe. In Germany, it goes like this: essentially you walk through the town in the freezing cold (which helps illustrate the moment when Saint Martin gave his coat to a poor beggar), following a rider on a horse (representing Martin), while small children hold lanterns and sing songs about the Saint. The procession has a police escort, and people play musical instruments along the route. At the end, there is a large bonfire and hot drinks for everyone. It may help you knowing the words of the children song:

Ich geh mit meiner Laterne

Und meine Laterne mit mir.

Da oben leuchten die Sterne

Und unten leuchten wir.

Mein Licht ist aus, Ich geh nach Haus,

Rabimmel, rabammel, rabum.

Laterne, Laterne,

Sonne, Mond und Sterne,

Brenne auf, mein Licht,

Brenne auf, mein Licht,

Aber nur meine liebe Laterne nicht.

Loriot

One of the most popular German comedians Vicco von Bülow, was better known by his stage name Loriot. Born in 1923 as Bernhard Victor Christoph-Carl von Bülow to a military officer in the Prussian town of Brandenburg on the Havel, he later took Loriot, French for oriole, as his stage name because the bird was his family's ancestral mascot. Exposing the canard of Germany as a humour-challenged place, Bülow was beloved for his television sketch comedy blending pratfalls with dry wit and was a fixture in German living rooms for decades. An amiable gentleman of aristocratic heritage with a keen sense of the absurd, Loriot frequently played the pompous fool, often with actress Evelyn Hamann as his foil. A household name in Germany since the 1950s, Loriot found success in film, theatre, publishing as well as television. He made his start drawing bulb-nosed cartoon characters, as well as whimsical dog and elephant figures called Wum and Wendelin, which he developed for the ZDF public television programme "The Big Prize." His comics and satirical prose, published by Diogenes, sold millions in German-speaking Europe, and he scored two box office smashes with movies he wrote and directed - "Ödipussi", about a man with an unhealthy attachment to his mother, and "Pappa ante Portas." Fans say his sense of the farcical in daily life always managed to touch a nerve.

Nena

German pop singer Nena made a big splash in the 1980s with *99 Luftballons*. After that worldwide hit, her career leveled off, especially in the non-German-speaking world. But in 2005 Nena released a new CD album that brought her back into the spotlight. Several songs from her "willst du mit mir gehn" CD, recorded in Berlin, Nena's adopted hometown, shot up in the German radio charts. Nena was born in Hagen, in the German region of Westphalia. After a short stint with a German band known as Stripes, she recorded her first hit, "Nur geträumt" ("only dreamed") in 1982.

Oktoberfest

Fall isn't fall without Oktoberfest!

The world's biggest beer festival has become a celebration of international stature: over six million visitors a year gather in Munich's famed Theresienwiese for 16 days of revelry and mini-Oktoberfests take place the world over. The most popular trade show on earth began with the wedding of Prince Ludwig and Princess Theresa of Bavaria in 1810. The royal nuptials just happened to coincide with the harvest and the tapping of the new brew, so the celebration was on permanently. Since 1818 Oktoberfest has been an official celebration in the beer capital of the world, and what a celebration it is!

The festivities are opened annually by parade of colorfully bedecked, horse drawn beer wagons and the inevitable marching bands, followed by men and women in traditional Bavarian garb, lederhosen and dirndls who animate spectators as they go along. The party officially begins at the stroke of noon, when Munich's mayor taps the first barrel of new beer. It's not surprising that Munich's Oktoberfest revelers imbibe about five million liters of that city's most famous product in the two-week period, but they're a hungry group too. Hundreds of thousands of chicken, oxen and sausages roast on spits throughout the city, and 45 million tons of fish are grilled.

Most importantly, remember to say, *Prost*! or "Cheers!"

Otto von Bismarck (1815–1898)

The unification of Germany under Prussian supremacy was the avowed aim of Otto von Bismarck, whom King Wilhelm I. had appointed Prime Minister of Prussia in 1862. Following the 1866 war against Austria, the German Confederation was dis¬ solved and replaced by the North German Confederation, which comprised 17 small German states under Prussian leadership. The victory over France in 1870/1 led to the foundation of the Second German Reich and the proclamation in Versailles of Wilhelm I as German Emperor. Bismarck remained Prime Minister and also became Reich Chancellor. The Reichstag was restructured as the people's elected representation, albeit with restricted rights. Bismarck led a bitter fight against leftwing liberalism, political Catholicism and social democracy, but in the 1880s was also responsible for the most progressive welfare legislation in the whole of Europe. Conflicts with Emperor Wilhelm II, who had been in power since 1888, led in 1890 to the dismissal of the "Iron Chancellor".

Sylt

The most expensive aggregation of sand and marram grass in the North Sea, Sylt makes an unlikely celeb heaven.

On the map, the 40km-long island of Sylt, just south of the Danish border, appears like a badly dented glider trying to fly towards England, but with its string still tied to the mainland. On the ground, the low-slung chic retreat turns out to be a giant sandbar with restaurants, with a fine sandy beach that runs the length of its 40km wingspan, backed by a fuselage of dunes, heather and a wig of grass. The string that secures this 'St Tropez of the North' to the mainland is a railway track, as there is no access road.

Never mind that this is not the Med. The temperamental North Sea weather is prized by the Sylterati (Bridget Bardot was here, as were artist Kandinsky and author Thomas Mann), who believe that soft sea air is better for the skin than any nourishing face creams. At its best, it's the Teutonic equivalent of Martha's Vineyard, with atmospheric sand dunes, lighthouses, reed-thatched cottages that house Hugo Boss and Louis Vuitton boutiques. Basic groceries are harder to find here than monogrammed luggage, and several of the restaurants are very highly rated in German foodie magazines. Fortunately the sunsets are more democratic, accessible to all. An exhilarating place to be when the weather is bad; an intoxicating place when the party crowd is in town. And outside July and August, it is calm, serene, inexpensive and accessible to all.

Tatort – German TV is murder

During the waning days of the Cold War, I liked to joke that if the Russians wanted to invade, they should do it on New Year's Eve. This was because everyone in the country was setting off loud firecrackers while completely drunk. Now having lived there for a decade, I've discovered an even better time to catch the Germans completely off guard: 8:15 pm on a Sunday. That's when the seminal Teutonic television crime-drama *Tatort*, or "Crime Scene," airs. At 39, *Tatort* is older than several members of Chancellor Angela Merkel's cabinet. It's probably one of the longest-running television shows on the planet and no self-respecting German would miss an episode.

Though I'd heard my friends talk about *Tatort* for years, its downmarket intro long turned me off. However, I was eventually lured in by the show's structure – each episode is set in a town or city with familiar detectives scattered throughout Germany. In Munich, a guy named Udo Wachtveitl plays a big-city Bavarian cop alongside partner Miroslav Nemec, who represents Germany's sizable Croatian population. In Bremen, Sabine Postel is a brash single mother and detective alongside Oliver Mommsen's run-of-the-mill cop who gets along better with his partner than his love interests. The regional structure isn't accidental. It reflects the country's network of public broadcasters, who also produce the episodes in their corner of the country. This adds background texture to the shows, such as the Baltic Sea and dairy cows playing a supporting role in Kiel just as the Rhine and *Kölsch* beer do in Cologne. The show's uneven scriptwriting is also an apt reflection of life in Germany – mostly mundane, sometimes gloomy and often just goofy. The singing detectives in Hamburg, for instance, were massively popular but made "Murder She Wrote" seem like a Salman Rushdie novel. Luckily they've since gone off the air. Still, most *Tatort* episodes are forgettable pulp, which makes them perfect couchtime companions. The show has also always reflected German societal issues of the day. Integrating the country's Turkish population, for example.

Tchibo

Tchibo is a German chain of coffee shops and cafés, also known for its weekly-changing range of other products. The latter includes: clothing, household items, electronics and electrical appliances. In Germany, Tchibo's slogan is "Every week a new world" (German: *Jede Woche eine neue Welt*). Recently Tchibo expanded its product range, and is now selling services such as travel and insurance. With over 1000 shops, Tchibo is one of Germany's biggest shop chains. The company is based in Hamburg. The name Tchibo is an abbreviation for Tchilling and Bohnen (beans, i.e. coffee beans).

Thomas "Thommy" Gottschalk

Unless you live in German-speaking Europe, Thomas Gottschalk is the host of the most famous TV show you've never heard of. Although he has appeared in a handful of German and Hollywood movies, Gottschalk is best known as the moderator and "Showmaster" of Europe's most successful television show of all time. Each airing of *Wetten, dass...?* "Wanna bet?" draws as many as 15 million viewers when it is broadcast from various German and European cities. But the famous TV star got his start in radio. It is difficult to describe his TV show or to compare Gottschalk's fame to American circumstances. As the show's host, Gottschalk has welcomed not only famous German entertainers and prominent politicians, but many international celebrities, including Madonna, Elton John, Shania Twain, Michael Jackson, and Green Day. His two-hour show, broadcast from a different city each time, is a sort of combination of "The Tonight Show" and "Beat the Clock."

There is nothing remotely like it on American TV, yet many American stars (Cameron Diaz, Catherine Zeta-Jones, Kevin Costner, Faith Hill, Carlos Santana) have appeared on *Wetten, dass..?* In Germany he is as famous as Jay Leno or David Letterman are in the US. It was his megastar status in Germany, Austria, and Switzerland that prompted Gottschalk to move his wife and two sons to southern California in 1987; the same year he began hosting the *Wetten, dass...?* show. He bought his first home in the Hollywood Hills with money from his first German McDonald's TV commercial. In Los Angeles and Malibu, the German celebrity and his family can enjoy a level of anonymity and freedom that is impossible in his homeland. Gottschalk also hosted a late night show on television, *Gottschalk Late Night* that featured the *Model '92 Competition*, in which Heidi Klum was the winner and received a modeling contract and winning prize, paving the way for her modeling career.

Willy Brandt

The Social Democrat was Chancellor of the Federal Republic from 1969 until 1974. In 1971, Brandt was awarded the Nobel Peace prize for his policy of Ostpolitik, which aimed to promote entente and political balance with East European states (the "policy of small steps"). His policy of detente contributed to the emergence of the Organization for Security and Cooperation in Europe (OSCE).

Women German football players

Women's football, gained a lot of publicity in Germany during the last World Cup in Germany. Germany's female national teams have done very well over the years and most Germans are aware of this.

TOPIC INDEX

Documenta

The Documenta in Kassel is the world's most important contemporary art exhibition. Founded on the initiative of painter Arnold Bode, it was first held in 1955, and then every five years for 100 days. The show was swiftly a world success, and will take place for the 13th time in 2012.

Economic miracle

The term "economic miracle" refers to West Germany's swift economic recovery following the Second World War. The prerequisites were the reconstruction of production facilities to the highest technical standards, the introduction of the deutschmark and massive financial support on the part of the USA through the Marshall Plan. By the late 1950s Germany had emerged as one of the leading economic nations.

Euro

The euro is the currency of the European Monetary Union and after the US dollar the second most important member of the international currency system. Together with the national central banks, the European Central Bank (ECB), headquartered in Frankfurt/Main, is responsible for monetary policy with regard to the euro. The euro is the official currency in 16 of the 27 EU member states. The euro was physically introduced in "Euroland", including Germany, on January 1, 2002, having served as a currency of deposit since the beginning of 1999.

Exports

Since 1991, the ratio of exports booked by the key exporting sectors has risen appreciably, testifying to German companies' strong competitive edge. Despite the economic crisis, in 2008 the export ratio in the mechanical engineering sector was 75 percent. In 1991 this figure stood at a mere 52 percent. In the chemicals and pharmaceuticals industry it rose from 50 percent to 79 percent, in the automobile industry from 43 percent to 74 percent, and in the electrical industry from 31 to 46 percent. The overall export ratio comes to almost 40 percent and as much as 47 percent if service exports are included. Germany's share of total world trade stands at nine percent.

Federal Chancellor

The Federal Chancellor is elected by the Bundestag after being proposed by the Federal President. The Federal Chancellor then proposes to the Federal President which ministers should be appointed. The Federal Chancellor heads the Federal Government in keeping with rules of procedure authorized by the Federal President. He bears responsibility for the Government vis-à-vis the Bundestag and in the case of national defence is supreme commander of the German Armed Forces.

Federal Government

The Federal Government and cabinet is made up of the Federal Chancellor and the Federal Ministers. While the Chancellor holds the power to issue directives, the ministers have departmental powers, meaning that they independently run their respective ministries in the framework of those directives. Moreover, the cabinet abides by the collegial principle, in disputes the Federal Government decides by majority. The affairs of state are managed by the Chancellor.

Federal state

The Federal Republic of Germany consists of 16 federal states. The powers of the state are divided up between government as a whole, the Federal Government and the federal states. The latter have independent, if limited government authority.

Fraunhofer-Gesellschaft

The society is engaged in applied research. Its projects are commissioned by industry and service providers as well as state-run institutions. Some 17,000 members of staff are employed in around 82 research facilities, including 60 Fraunhofer institutes throughout the whole of Germany. The amount spent on research annually totals EUR 1.5 billion. Fraunhofer supports offices in Europe, the USA, Asia, and the Middle East.

Helmholtz Association

With 16 research centers, an annual budget of around EUR 2.8 billion and 28,000 members of staff the Helmholtz Association is Germany's largest scientific organization. It conducts research into energy, the earth and the environment, health, key technologies, the structure of material as well as traffic and outer space.

International Frankfurt Book Fair

The International Frankfurt Book Fair has taken place every autumn since 1949 and is the outstanding annual international book trade get-together. The highpoint of every book fair is the award-giving ceremony for the Peace Prize of the German Book Trade, which has been won by the likes of Václav Havel, Jorge Semprún and Susan Sontag. Since 2005, to mark the beginning of the Book Fair, the German Book Prize is presented for the best novel written in German.

ISAF

The German army, the Bundeswehr, has been part of the International Security Assistance Force (ISAF) for

Afghanistan since 2002. The deployment of ISAF is a military mission. With its rulings of April 1993 and June 1994 the Federal Constitutional Court cleared the path for deployment by the German Armed Forces on such missions as well; since December 2004 the Act on Parliamentary Participation on Decisions to Deploy Armed Forces Abroad sets out the Bundestag's powers in such cases. Today, under a UN mandate the ISAF supports the government of Afghanistan in training Afghan security forces, protecting the population, and creating a safe environment for civil reconstruction.

Leibniz Association

Gottfried Wilhelm Leibniz (1646–1716) was one of the last all-round scholars. The scientific range covered by the 86 member institutes is correspondingly broad, extending from the humanities and economics through to mathematics. The focus is on applied basic research. The Leibniz institutes employ more than 14,000 staff and have a total budget of over EUR 1 billion.

Max Planck Society

The Max Planck Society was founded on February 26, 1948 – as the successor to the Kaiser Wilhelm Society set up in 1911 for the promotion of science. Max Planck Institutes undertake basic research in the natural sciences, bio-sciences and social sciences as well as the humanities. Together with partner universities, MPG has founded 55 postgraduate and international Max Planck Research Schools. Half of the doctoral students come from outside Germany.

News agencies

Deutsche Presse-Agentur (dpa) is the largest German news agency. Alongside AFP, Reuters and AP it is one of the leading international agencies.

Reunification

Following the peaceful overthrow of the East German regime in 1989, reunification of the two Germanys moved that step closer. In the summer of 1990 negotiations about the reunification treaty commenced in Berlin. On October 3, 1990 on the basis of Article 23 of the Basic Law, East Germany acceded to the territory of the Federal Republic of Germany. On December 2, 1990 the first all-German elections to the Bundestag took place.

Standard of qualification

Some 50 percent of young people go into vocational training for a state-recognized profession either on the dual vocational training system or as school training in a vocational college. 45 percent of this age group acquires the right to study. In terms of total numbers the ratio of students beginning a degree course is 43 of an academic year

The Alexander von Humboldt Foundation

The Alexander von Humboldt Foundation was founded in 1860 and today promotes academic collaboration between excellent foreign and German researchers. Every year it enables 1,900 international researchers to spend time working in Germany and maintains a worldwide network of some 23,000 Humboldtians from all disciplines in 130 countries – including 43 Nobel Prize winners.

University ranking

Oldest university:

Ruprecht Karls University, Heidelberg, founded in 1386

Biggest university:

Ludwig Maximilians University, Munich, with 44.400 students

Most attractive university for top international research:

Technical University, Munich, according to the Alexander von Humboldt Foundation-based research ranking

Universities with greatest research activities:

Rwth Aachen University, according to the promotion ranking of the German Research Foundation.

WEB LINKS

www.thelocal.de

In brief, The Local Web site is for anyone who is interested in finding out what's going on in Germany and who reads English. I discovered it when I lived in Stockholm for the Swedish version, and luckily in the meanwhile it has been created a German version.

www.deutschland.de

Official portal of the Federal Republic of Germany. It provides access in Arabic, English, French, German, Russian, and Spanish to link lists for all areas of society

www.bundesregierung.de

The comprehensive German federal government Web site, including topical news on government policies (English, French and German)

www.auswaertiges-amt.de

Information on aspects of German foreign policy and addresses of the German missions abroad (Arabic, English, French, German and Spanish)

www.gtai.de

The Web site of the federal agency Invest in Germany GmbH provides information on Germany as a business hub (in six languages)

www.auma.de

AUMA offers information about the trade show industry and a worldwide trade show data base (German, English, French and Spanish)

www.bmwi.de

The Federal Ministry of Economics and Technology Web site provides comprehensive information on the topic (German, English, French)

www.german-business-portal.info

This service offered by the BMWI specifically targets international interested parties (English)

www.ahk.de

The website of the German Chamber network provides information for German companies planning to invest abroad (English, German)

www.goethe.de

The Goethe-Institut Web site provides information on language courses and events at the 142 institutes as well as on German culture and society (English and German)

www.ifa.de

The Institut für Auslandsbeziehungen (ifa) offers an overview of topics relating to international cultural exchange (English, German, Portuguese and Spanish)

www.daad.de

The German Academic Exchange Service (DAAD) provides information on funding and exchange programs for students, graduates and scientists (in 22 languages)

www.dw-world.de

German foreign broadcasting station Deutsche Welle (DW) provides a wealth of topical editorial information (in 30 languages)

www.deutschland-tourismus.de

The German National Tourist Board Web site offers a wide range of details on Germany as a holiday destination (English and German)

www.land-der-ideen.de

The "Germany. Land of Ideas" initiative champions Germany as a center and, among other things, runs a special media service (English and German)

www.destatis.de

Web site of the German Federal Statistical Office (English and German)

www.magazine-deutschland.de

Web site of "Deutschland" magazine, with articles on current topics, a service section and a media corner for journalists (in ten languages)